Primary Geography

Teacher's Book 5 Change

Stephen Scoffham | Colin Bridge

Geography in the primary school

Geography is the study of the Earth's surface. It helps children understand the human and physical forces which shape the environment. Children are naturally interested in their immediate surroundings. They also want to know about places beyond their direct experience. Geography is uniquely placed to satisfy this curiosity.

Geographical enquiries

Geography is an enquiry-led subject that seeks to answer fundamental questions such as:

- Where is this place?
- What is this place like (and why)?
- How and why is it changing?
- How does this place compare with other places?
- How and why are places connected?

These questions involve not only finding out about the natural processes which have shaped our environment, they also involve finding out how people have responded to them. Studying this interaction at a range of scales from the local to the global and asking questions about what is happening in the world around us lie at the heart of both academic and school geography.

Geographical perspectives

Geographical perspectives offer a uniquely powerful way of seeing the world. Since the time of the Ancient Greeks geographers have been attempting to chronicle and interpret their surroundings. One way of seeing links and connections is to think in terms of key ideas. Three concepts which geographers have found particularly useful in a range of settings are place, space and scale.

- Place focuses attention on the environment.
- Space focuses attention on location.
- Scale introduces a change in perspective that enables us to link the local and the global.

A layer of secondary concepts such as patterns, change and movement lie beneath these fundamental organising ideas and provide a way of further enhancing our understanding.

As they conduct their enquiries and investigations geographers make use of a number of specific skills. Foremost among these are mapwork and the ability to represent spatial information. The use of maps, charts, diagrams, tables, sketches and other cartographic techniques come under the more general heading of 'graphicacy' and are a distinguishing feature of geographical thinking. As more and more information has come to be represented electronically, the use of computers and other electronic applications has been championed by geography educators.

Geography in primary schools offers children from the earliest ages a fascinating window onto the contemporary world. The challenge for educators is to find ways of providing experiences and selecting content that will help children develop an increasingly deep understanding.

Collins Primary Geography

Collins Primary Geography is a complete programme for pupils in the primary school and can be used as a structure for teaching geography from ages 5-11. It consists of five pupil books and supporting teacher's guides with notes and copymasters. There is one pupil book at Key Stage 1 and four pupil books at Key Stage 2. There is also a supporting DVD for each Key Stage.

Aims

The overall aim of the programme is to inspire children with an enthusiasm for geography and to empower them as learners. The underlying principles include a commitment to international understanding in a more equitable world, a concern for the future welfare of the planet and a recognition that creativity, hope and optimism play a fundamental role in lasting learning. Three different dimensions – connecting to the environment, connecting to each other and connecting to ourselves – are explored throughout the programme in different contexts and at a range of scales. We believe that learning to think geographically in the broadest meaning of the term will help children make wise decisions in the future as they grow into adulthood.

Structure

Collins Primary Geography provides full coverage of the English National Curriculum requirements. Each pupil book covers a balanced range of themes and topics and includes case studies with a more precise focus:

- Book 1 and 2 *World around us* introduces pupils to the world at both a local and global scale.
- Book 3 *Investigation* encourages pupils to conduct their own research and enquiries.
- Book 4 *Movement* considers how movement affects the physical and human environment.
- Book 5 *Change* includes case studies on how places alter and develop.
- Book 6 *Issues* introduces more complex ideas to do with the environment and sustainability.

Although the books are not limited to a specific year band, Book 3 will be particularly suitable for Year 3 children. Similarly, Book 4 is focused on Year 4 children. However it is also possible to trace themes from one book to another. The programme is structured in such a way that key themes are revisited making it possible to investigate a specific topic in greater depth if required.

Investigations

Enquiries and investigations are an important part of pupils' work in primary geography. Asking questions and searching for answers can help children develop key knowledge, understanding and skills. Fieldwork is time consuming when it involves travelling to distant locations, but local area work can be equally effective. Many of the exercises in *Collins Primary Geography* focus on the classroom, school building and local environment. We believe that such activities can have a seminal role in promoting long term positive attitudes towards sustainability and the environment.

Places, themes and skills

Each book is divided into ten units giving a balance between places, themes and skills.

Places

There are locality studies throughout each book and studies of specific places from the UK, Europe and other continents. These studies illustrate how people interact with their physical surroundings in a constantly changing world. The places have been selected so that by the end of the scheme, children will be familiar with a balanced range of reference points from around the world. They should also have developed an increasingly sophisticated locational framework which will enable them to place their new knowledge in context.

Themes

Physical geography is covered in the initial three units of each book which focus on planet Earth, water and weather. Human geography is considered in units on settlements, work and travel. There is also a unit specifically devoted to the urban and rural environment and human impact on the natural world. This is a very important aspect of modern geography and a key topic for schools generally.

Skills

Maps and plans are introduced in context to convey information about the places which are being studied. The books contain maps at scales which range from the local to global and use a range of techniques which children can emulate. Charts, diagrams and other graphical devices are included throughout. Fieldwork is strongly emphasised and all the books include projects and investigations which can be conducted in the local environment.

Information technology

Geography has always been closely associated with information technology. The way in which computers can be used for recording and processing information is illustrated in each of the books. Satellite images are included together with information from data handling packages. Oblique and vertical aerial photographs are included as sources of evidence.

Cross-curricular links

The different units in *Collins Primary Geography* can be easily linked with other subjects. The physical geography units have natural synergies with themes from sciences, as do the units on the environment. Local area studies overlap with work in history. Furthermore, the opportunities for promoting the core subjects are particularly strong. Each lesson is supported by discussion questions and many of the investigations involve written work in different modes and registers.

Places, themes and skills

Places and Themes	Book 3 Units	Book 4 Units	Book 5 Units	Book 6 Units
Planet Earth	Landscapes	Coasts	Seas and oceans	Restless Earth
Water	Water around us	Rivers	Wearing away the land	Drinking water
Weather	Weather worldwide	Weather patterns	The seasons	Local weather
Settlements	Villages	Towns	Cities	Planning issues
Work and travel	Travel	Food and shops	Jobs	Transport
Environment	Caring for the countryside	Caring for towns	Pollution	Conservation
United Kingdom	Scotland	Northern Ireland	Wales	England
Europe	France	Germany	Greece	Europe
North and South America	South America *Chile*	North America *The Rocky Mountains*	North America *Jamaica*	South America *The Amazon*
Asia and Africa	Asia *India*	Asia *UAE*	Africa *Kenya*	Asia *Singapore*

Layout of the units

Each book is divided into ten units composed of three lessons. In the opening units pupils are introduced to key themes such as water, weather, settlement and the environment at increasing levels of complexity. The following units focus on places from around the UK, Europe and other continents. The overall aim is to provide a balanced coverage of geography.

Unit title
Identifies the focus of the unit and suggests links and connections to other subjects.

Graphics
Graphical devices ranging from maps to satellite images amplify the topic.

Lesson title
Identifies the theme of the lesson. The supporting copymaster also uses this title which makes it easy to identify.

Data Bank
Provides extra information to engage children and encourage them to find out more for themselves.

Enquiry question
Suggests opportunities for open-ended investigations and practical activities.

Mapwork exercise
Indicates how the lesson can be developed through atlas and mapwork.

Key word panel
Highlights key geographical words and terms which will be used during the lesson.

Investigation panel
Suggests a practical activity which will help pupils consolidate their understanding.

Introductory text
Introduces the topic in a graded text of around 100 words.

Summary panel
Indicates the knowledge and understanding covered in the unit.

Discussion panel
Consists of three questions designed to draw pupils into the topic and to stimulate discussion. The first question often involves simple comprehension, the second question involves reasoning and the third question introduces a human element which helps to relate the topic to the child's own experience.

Copymasters
Each lesson has a supporting copymaster which can be found in pages 30-59 of this book.

Layout of the units

Enquiry question

Lesson title

Unit title

Key word panel

Mapwork exercise

Lesson 2: World cities

How are cities changing?

Around the world, many cities are getting bigger as people move in from the countryside. Some people are attracted to cities because they think they will find a better life there. Others are forced to move out of their villages by war, drought and famine.

Key words
city
countryside
population

City	Millions of people 1980	Millions of people 2020 (estimate)
Tokyo, Japan	29	39
Delhi, Inda	6	29
Shanghai, China	6	26
Mumbai, India	9	24
Mexico City, Mexico	13	23
New York, USA	16	22
São Paulo, Brazil	12	22
Beijing, China	5	21
Dhaka, Bangladesh	3	20
Karachi, Pakistan	5	18
Kolkata, India	9	17
Lagos, Nigeria	3	16

Discussion
- Which will be the three largest cities in the world in 2020?
- Why do cities attract people?
- What is special about the city nearest to you?

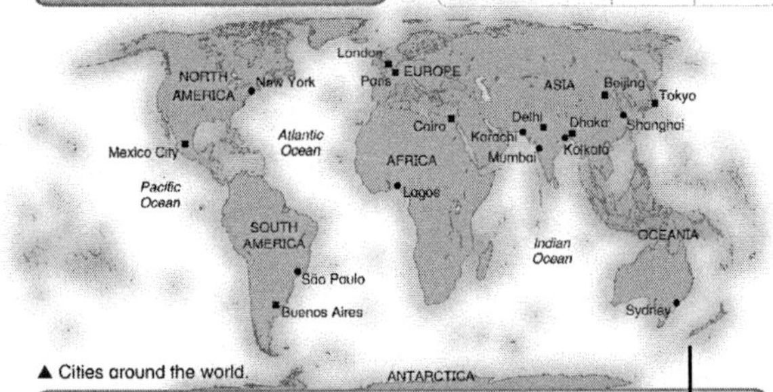

▲ Cities around the world.

Investigation
Using the data from the world cities table above draw a bar chart of the world's city populations.

22

The story of New York

New York is on the east coast of the United States of America. It began as a trading post set up by Dutch sailors nearly 400 years ago. Now it has a population of 20 million people speaking 800 languages and is an important centre for world trade and finance.

New York is famous for the Statue of Liberty and the Empire State Building. Central Park is a popular meeting place. The museums of modern art and natural history attract many visitors. In the evening there are shows to see in the 40 theatres along Broadway.

New York enjoys sunshine on most days in the year but January can be very cold and sudden deep snow is not unusual.

Mapwork
Using the internet, make your own simple sketch map of central New York.

Data Bank
- The Empire State Building has 102 floors and 6500 windows.
- In New York, people spend over one billion dollars on theatre tickets each year.
- There are 70 000 helicopter flights over New York each year.

▲ Central New York.

23

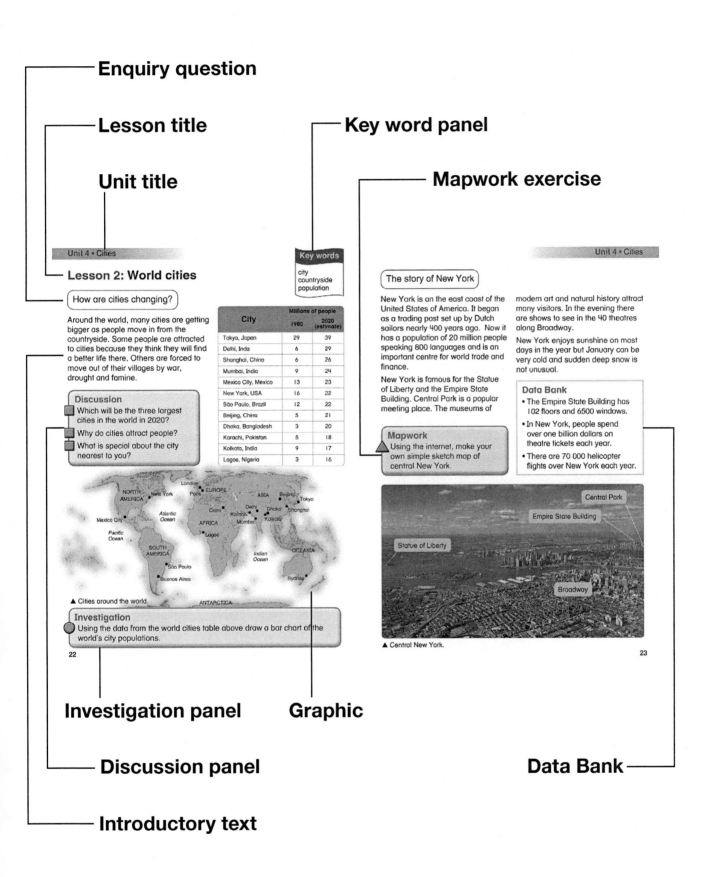

Investigation panel

Graphic

Discussion panel

Data Bank

Introductory text

Lesson planning

Collins Primary Geography has been designed to support both whole school and individual lesson planning. As you devise your schemes and work out lesson plans you may find it helpful to ask the following questions. For example, have you:

- Given children a range of entry points which will engage their enthusiasm and capture their imagination?
- Used a range of teaching strategies which cater for pupils who learn in different ways?
- Thought about using games as a teaching device?
- Explored the ways that stories or personal accounts might be integrated with the topic?
- Considered the opportunities for practical activities and fieldwork enquiries?
- Encouraged pupils to use globes and maps where appropriate?
- Considered whether to include a global dimension?
- Checked to see whether you are challenging rather than reinforcing stereotypes?
- Checked on links to suitable websites, particularly with respect to research?
- Made use of ICT to record findings or analyse information?

- Made links to other subjects where there is a natural overlap?
- Promoted geography alongside literacy skills especially in talking and writing?
- Taken advantage of the opportunities for presentations and class displays?
- Ensured that the pupils are developing geographical skills and meaningful subject knowledge?
- Clarified the knowledge, skills and concepts that will underpin the unit?
- Identified appropriate learning outcomes or given pupils the opportunity to identify their own ones?

These questions are offered as prompts which may help you to generate stimulating and lively lessons. There is clear evidence that when geography is fun and pupils enjoy what they are doing it can lead to lasting learning. Striking a balance between light-hearted delivery and serious intent is part of the craft of being a teacher.

Misconceptions

There is a growing body of research which helps practitioners to understand more about how children learn primary geography and the barriers and challenges that they commonly encounter. The way that young children assume that the physical environment was created by people was first highlighted by Jean Piaget. The importance and significance of early childhood misconceptions was further illuminated by Howard Gardner. More recent research has considered how children develop their understanding of maps and places. Children's ideas about other countries and their attitudes to other nationalities form another very important line of enquiry. Some key readings are listed in the references on page 15.

Lesson summary

The table below provides an overview of the lessons in *Collins Primary Geography Pupil Book 5*. Individual schools may want to adapt the lessons and associated activities according to their particular needs and circumstances.

Theme	Unit	Lesson 1	Lesson 2	Lesson 3
Planet Earth	Seas and oceans	Beneath the surface	The ocean environment	Learning about seas
Water	Wearing away the land	Rivers in action	Preventing flood damage	Finding out about rivers
Weather	The seasons	Changing seasons	Seasons worldwide	Seasonal influences
Settlements	Cities	Describing cities	World cities	The story of London
Work and travel	Jobs	Making things	Different jobs	Types of work
Environment	Pollution	Damaging the environment	'Green living'	Exploring clean energy
United Kingdom	Wales	Mountains and valleys	The story of Blaenavon	A visit to Big Pit
Europe	Greece	Introducing Greece	Summer in Athens	A Greek island
North and South America	North America	Introducing the Caribbean	Finding out about Jamaica	Living in Jamaica
Asia and Africa	Africa	Introducing Africa	Kenya	Living in Kenya

Studying the local area

The local area is the immediate vicinity around the school and the home. It consists of three different components: the school building, the school grounds, and local streets and buildings. By studying their local area, children will learn about the different features which make their environment distinctive and how it attains a specific character. When they are familiar with their own area, they will then be able to make meaningful comparisons with more distant places.

There are many opportunities to support the lessons outlined in *Collins Primary Geography* with practical local area work. First-hand experience is fundamental to good practice in geography teaching, is a clear requirement in the programme of study and has been highlighted in guidance to Ofsted inspectors. The local area can be used not only to develop ideas from human geography but also to illustrate physical and environmental themes. The checklist below illustrates some of the features which could be identified and studied.

Physical geography	Human geography
Hill, valley, cliff, mountain, rock, slope, soil, wood	Origins of settlements, land use and economic activity
River, stream, pond, lake, estuary, coast	House, cottage, terrace, flat, housing estate
Slopes, rock, soil, plants and other small-scale features	Roads, stations, harbours
Local weather and site conditions	Shops, factories and offices
	Fire, police, ambulance, health services
	Library, museum, park, leisure centre

All work in the local area involves collecting and analysing information. An important way in which this can be achieved is through the use of maps and plans. Other techniques include annotated drawings, bar charts, tables and reports. There will also be opportunities for the children to make presentations in class and perhaps to the rest of the school in assemblies

Studying places in the UK and wider world

Collins Primary Geography Pupil Book 5 contains studies of the following places in the UK and wider world. Place studies focus on small scale environments and everyday life. By considering people and describing their surroundings, the information is presented at a scale and in a manner which relates particularly well to children. Research shows that pupils tend to reach a peak of friendliness towards other countries and nations at about the age of ten. It is important to capitalise on this educationally and to challenge prejudices and stereotypes.

Pennines
p.18

Whitby
p.19

Blaenavon
pp.40-41

London
pp.24-25

Devon
pp.12-13

NORTH AMERICA

Jamaica
pp.52-55

Wales
pp.38-43

UK

EUROPE

Greece
pp.44-49

ASIA

Atlantic Ocean

AFRICA

Kenya
pp.58-61

Pacific Ocean

Indian Ocean

OCEANIA

SOUTH AMERICA

Southern Ocean

ANTARCTICA

Differentiation and progression

Collins Primary Geography sets out to provide access to the curriculum for children of all abilities. It is structured so that children can respond to and use the material in a variety of ways. Within each unit there is a range of exercises and discussion questions. This means activities can be selected which are appropriate to individual circumstances.

Differentiation by outcome

Each lesson starts with an introductory text and linked discussion questions which are designed to capture the children's imagination and draw them into the topic. There are opportunities for slower learners to relate the material to their own experience. More able children will be able to consider the underlying geographical concepts. The pace and range of the discussion can be controlled to suit the needs of the class or group.

Differentiation by process

Children of all abilities benefit from exploring their environment and conducting their own investigations. The investigation activities include many suggestions for direct experience and first-hand learning. Work in the local area can overcome the problems of written communication by focusing on concrete events. There are also opportunities for taking photographs and conducting surveys as well as for making lists, diagrams and written descriptions.

Differentiation by task

The mapwork and investigation exercises can be modified according to the pupils' ability levels. Teachers may decide to complete some of the tasks as class exercises or help slower learners by working through the first part of an exercise with them. Classroom assistants could also use the lessons with individual children or small groups. More able children could be given extension tasks. Ideas and suggestions for extending each lesson are provided in the information on individual units (pages 16-25).

Progression

The themes, language and complexity of the material have been graded to provide progression between each title. However, the gradient between different books is deliberately shallow. This makes it possible for the books to be used interchangeably by different year groups or within mixed ability classes. The way that this might work can be illustrated by considering a sample unit. For instance, in Book 3 the unit on weather introduces children to hot and cold places around the world. Book 4 looks at ways of recording the weather, Book 5 focuses on the seasons and Book 6 considers local weather conditions. This approach provides opportunities for reinforcement and revisiting which will be particularly helpful for the less able child.

Assessment

Assessment is often seen as having two very different dimensions. Formative assessment is an on-going process which provides both pupils and teachers with information about the progress they are making in a piece of work. Summative assessment occurs at defined points in a child's learning and seeks to establish what they have learnt and how they are performing in relation both to their peers and to nationally agreed standards. *Collins Primary Geography* provides opportunities for both formative and summative assessment.

Formative assessment

- The discussion questions invite pupils to discuss a topic, relate it to their previous experience and consider any issues which may arise, thereby yielding information about their current knowledge and understanding.
- The mapwork exercises focus especially on developing spatial awareness and skills and will indicate the pupils' current level of ability
- The investigation activities give pupils the chance to extend their knowledge in ways that match their current abilities.

Summative assessment

- The panels at the end of each unit highlight key learning outcomes. These can be tested directly through individually designed exercises.
- The copymasters (see pages 30-59) can be used to provide additional evidence of pupil achievement. Whether used formatively or summatively they are intended to broaden and consolidate understanding.

Reporting to parents

Collins Primary Geography is structured around geographical skills, themes and place studies which become more complex from one book to another. As children work through the units they can build up a folder of work. This will include mapwork and investigations in the local area and will provide evidence of breadth, progression and achievement in geography. It will also be a useful resource when teachers report to parents about whether an individual child is above average, satisfactory, or in need of help in geography.

National curriculum reporting

There is a single attainment target for geography and other National Curriculum subjects. This simply states that

> *'By the end of each key stage, pupils are expected to know, apply and understand the matters, skills and processes specified in the relevant programme of study.'*

This means that assessment need not be an onerous burden and that evidence of pupils' achievement can be built up over an entire Key Stage. The assessment process can also inform lesson planning. Establishing what pupils have demonstrably understood helps to highlight more clearly what they still need to learn.

High quality geography

The regular reviews of geography teaching in the UK undertaken by Ofsted provide a clear guidance.

Ofsted recommendations
Ofsted recommends schools to:
- focus on developing pupils' core knowledge and sense of place.
- ensure that geography elements are clearly identified within topic based work.
- maximize opportunities for fieldwork in order to improve pupil motivation.
- make the most of new technology to enthuse pupils and provide immediacy and relevance.
- provide more opportunities for writing at length and focused reading.
- enable pupils to recognise their responsibilities as citizens.
- develop networks to share good practice.
- provide subject specific support and professional development opportunities for teachers.

Primary Geography Quality Mark
The Primary Geography Quality Mark set up by the UK Geographical Association is another measure of excellence. This provides a self-assessment framework designed to help subject leaders. There are three categories of award. The 'bronze' level recognises that lively and enjoyable geography is happening in your school, the 'silver' level recognises excellence across the school and the 'gold' level recognises excellence that is shared and embedded in the community beyond the school. The framework is divided into four separate cells (a) pupil progress and achievement (b) quality of teaching (c) behaviour and relationships (d) leadership and management. For further details see www.geography.org.uk.

Achieving accreditation for geography in school is a useful way of badging achievements and identifying targets for future improvement. The Geographical Association provides a wide range of support to help teachers with this process. In addition to an ambassador scheme and Continuing Professional Development (CPD) sessions it produces a journal for primary schools, *Primary Geography*, three time a year. Other key sources are the Geographical Association website, the *Primary Geography Handbook* and books and guides for classroom use such as *Geography Plus*.

Finding time for geography
The pressures on the school timetable and the demands of the core subjects make it hard to secure adequate time for primary geography. However, finding ways of integrating geography with mathematics and literacy can be a creative way of increasing opportunities. Geography also has a natural place in a wide range of social studies and current affairs whether local or global. It can be developed through class assemblies and extra-curricular studies. Those who are committed to thinking geographically find a surprising number of ways of developing the subject whatever the accountability regime in which they operate.

Ofsted inspections

Ofsted inspections are designed to monitor standards of teaching in schools in England and Wales. Curriculum development is an on-going process and inspectors do not always expect to see totally completed programmes. What they are looking for is evidence of carefully planned strategies which are having a positive impact on the quality of teaching. However, inspectors must also note weaknesses and highlight aspects which need attention. If curriculum development is already in hand in your school, it should receive positive support. The following checklist provides prompts which may help prepare for inspections.

1 Identify a teacher who is responsible for developing the geography curriculum.
2 Provide a regular opportunity for discussing geography teaching in staff meetings.
3 See that all members of staff are familiar with the geography curriculum.
4 Decide how geography will fit into your whole school plan.
5 Make an audit of current geography teaching resources to identify gaps and weaknesses.
6 Discuss and develop a geography policy which includes statements on overall aims, topic planning, teaching methods, resources, assessment and recording.
7 Discuss the policy with the governors.
8 Devise an action plan for geography which includes an annual review procedure.

References and further reading

Bonnett, A. (2009) *What is Geography?* London: Sage

Butt, G. (Ed.) (2011) *Geography, Education and the Future,* London: Continuum

Catling, S. and Willy, T. (2009) *Teaching Primary Geography,* Exeter: Learning Matters

DfE (2013) National Curriculum in England: Programmes of study – Key Stages 1 and 2 available at www.education.gov.uk/schools/teachingandlearning/curriculum/primary

Lucas, B. and Claxton, G. (2011) *New Kinds of Smart,* Maidenhead: Open University Press

Martin, F. (2006) *Teaching Geography in Primary Schools : Learning to live in the world,* Cambridge: Kington

Ofsted (2011) *Geography: Learning to Make a World of Difference,* London: Ofsted

Scoffham, S. (Ed.) (2010) *Primary Geography Handbook,* Sheffield: Geographical Association

Scoffham, S. (Ed.) (2013) *Teaching Geography Creatively,* London: Routledge

Wiegand, P. (2006) *Learning and Teaching with Maps,* London: Routledge

The Geographical Association

The Geographical Association (GA) provides extensive support and advice for teachers including a range of excellent publications such as the *Everyday Geography* and *Geography Plus* series. As well as holding an annual conference, the GA also produces a journal for primary practitioners, *Primary Geography*, which is published three times a year. To find out more and learn about the latest developments in geography education visit the website at www.geography.org.uk.

Unit 1: SEAS AND OCEANS

We tend to think of oceans as barriers because we live on dry land. Their vast size and depth makes them seem difficult to penetrate. The average depth is five kilometres which means that the oceans go down much deeper than the land rises up. In places, there are dramatic landscape features, such as underwater mountains, ridges and valleys.

We now know that the oceans play a major part in the global ecosystem. They stabilise the climate, balance the atmosphere and support a great variety of life. Recently, scientists have discovered new forms of life which feed on the sulphur and minerals that bubble out of volcanic vents. However it is also recognised that the oceans are becoming more acidic as they absorb atmospheric pollution. This may be masking the full impact of global warming.

Lesson 1: BENEATH THE SURFACE
What is it like under the oceans?

Most children will have no direct experience of the different plants and animals which live below the ocean surface. The drawing and photographs are designed to capture the children's imagination and encourage discussion. They also show the changes which occur with increasing depth. Below a few hundred metres it is almost completely dark, the water is just above freezing and the pressure begins to increase considerably. When the children think about their imaginary submarine journey they might mention the silence and feeling of loneliness in the ocean deeps.

Mapwork *The children should make drawings to show a cross section.*

Investigation *You might structure the class scrapbook around sea creatures in general, a specific ocean or get them to select one image for each letter of the alphabet.*

Lesson 2: THE OCEAN ENVIRONMENT
What are the threats to the ocean environment?

The photographs and text panels describe ways in which people exploit the oceans and also draw attention to environmental and conservation issues. Managing the ocean environment is complicated as it requires international agreement. Enforcing laws and agreements is another issue.

Mapwork *One way to show the Arctic Ocean is to use a polar projection with the North Pole at the centre of a circular map.*

Investigation *Encourage pupils to use maps and charts as well as drawings in their posters.*

Lesson 3: LEARNING ABOUT SEAS
What is a sea?

Many people use the term 'sea' and 'ocean' more or less interchangeably. However, not only are seas much smaller and shallower than oceans, but they are often partially enclosed.

Mapwork *The children should include bays, gulfs and other more specific types of sea in their lists.*

The North Sea

The case study of the North Sea was selected not only because it is fringes the east coast of the UK but because of the enormously different ways in which it is used.

Investigation *The North Sea supports a large number of marine mammals, millions of sea birds and is also home to cold water corals.*

Copymasters *See 1, 2 and 3 for linked extension exercises.*

Unit 2: WEARING AWAY THE LAND

Landscapes slowly take shape over very long periods of time due to weathering and erosion. Weathering is the breakdown of rocks and other materials in the place where they are found. Erosion is the removal of these materials by wind, water, gravity or ice.

Rivers play an important part in the process of erosion. The sheer force of the water as it flows downhill wears away the land. However, as rivers gather particles of rock, the water becomes much more abrasive and scrapes away at the sides and bottom of the channel. Further downstream, rivers deposit their load as mud and sediment.

Around the world people exploit rivers in different ways. Dams are particularly helpful in preventing floods and providing water to generate power and irrigate fields. However, controlling rivers is a complicated business which entails environmental and financial costs as well as benefits.

Lesson 1: RIVERS IN ACTION
How do rivers shape the land?

The photograph of the canoeist negotiating a rapid shows the force of the water as it cascades downhill. Rapids are usually caused by layers of hard rock which wear away more slowly than the surrounding areas of softer rock. This gives the river bottom a continuous slope, unlike waterfalls which have a vertical drop. Children often find it difficult to understand the idea of erosion, transportation and deposition. These are complex processes that happen very gradually. However, they can also be seen much more vividly in times of flood if large objects, such as trees and boulders, are carried downstream.

Investigation *Many of the terms which relate to rivers such 'source', 'channel' and 'mouth' are homonyms - words with more than one meaning. You might want to explain this to pupils so that they do not become confused.*

Lesson 2: PREVENTING FLOOD DAMAGE
How can we control rivers?

The Mississippi was chosen for this case study not only because it is a major world river, but because it also causes spectacular floods. Until recently many people believed that it was possible to control the Mississippi but now they are not sure. This reflects a change of attitude towards the environment.

Rather than seeking to dominate natural forces, environmentalists argue that we should work in harmony with them.

Mapwork *Note that the Missouri which rises in the Rockies joins the Mississippi at St Louis adding considerably to its length.*

Investigation *The investigation relates this topic to the pupil's own environment and circumstances and could be linked to local history.*

Lesson 3: Finding out about rivers
What data is needed to find out about a river?

The work done by St Mark's Primary School shows the educational potential of a river study. Even if you are unable to leave the classroom, the children can learn at secondhand from the account given here. If you do decide to conduct a fieldwork study, remember that heavy rain will swell water levels and may present dangers not considered in your original risk assessment.

Mapwork *This is a good opportunity to use a 1:50 000 Ordnance Survey map of your locality.*

Investigation *Each of the survey questions could be developed as a more substantial study if time permits.*

Copymasters *See 4, 5 and 6 for linked extension exercises.*

Unit 3: THE SEASONS

The seasons are caused by the movement of the Earth around the Sun and the tilt in the Earth's axis. In June, the North Pole is tilted towards the Sun creating summer in the northern hemisphere and winter in the southern hemisphere. In December, the North Pole is tilted away from the Sun and the seasons are reversed.

In very general terms, the world can be divided into three main climate regions. There are cold regions around the North and South Poles, hot regions around the Equator and temperate areas in between. The UK lies in the temperate area and has four distinct seasons. Seasons and climate have a dominant effect on plant and animal life. Even in the modern world, the seasons also influence the crops people can grow, the houses we live in and the clothes we wear.

Lesson 1: CHANGING SEASONS
What are the seasons?

Pupils need to understand that the seasons follow a pattern. There may be slight variations in individual years but over a period of time the overall character of each season is clearly identifiable. The charts, diagrams and photographs provide different but complementary information about seasonal change and its impact on natural life.

Mapwork *Although mapwork activities are not suggested for this spread pupils could research seasonal variations in the UK – the number of 'snow days' in different areas is particularly revealing.*

Investigation *Pupils could make individual seasons dials but you could also construct a large one as a class display.*

Lesson 2: SEASONS WORLDWIDE
Do all places have the same seasons?

Children often believe that all places have the same pattern of seasons as the UK. The case studies challenge this assumption. The Mediterranean climate was chosen as pupils may have been to southern Europe for their summer holidays. Southeast Asia offers a striking contrast to the Mediterranean – a quarter of the world's population depends on the monsoon rains for their survival.

Mapwork *Monsoon climates are sometimes grouped under the more general heading of 'tropical climate'. The key feature is a distinctive wet and dry season.*

Investigation *When pupils write their descriptions they could include the weather, plants and creatures as well as seasonal past-times.*

Lesson 3: SEASONAL INFLUENCES
How are farmers affected by the seasons?

Even though farmers try to overcome the weather, e.g. ploughing by night and keeping livestock indoors, the seasons still have a major impact on their lives.

Mapwork *Pupils might plan a walk for other seasons, depending on when they are doing the work.*

Investigation *Children might complete the seasons chart as a homework exercise, using their house and garden as the example.*

How are seaside resorts affected by the seasons?

Seasonal changes have a very significant impact on shops and businesses in seaside resorts. Whitby is representative of places all around the coast of the UK in this respect.

Copymasters *See 7, 8 and 9 for linked extension exercises.*

Unit 4: CITIES

The first cities were built thousands of years ago in the Middle East, Egypt and China. They depended on a settled system of agriculture which produced enough food to support an urban population. As people congregated together so art, politics, science and culture began to flourish. Today, cities dominate human affairs. For the first time in history more than half the world's population now live in built-up areas. Urban life brings many challenges. In the developing world, cities tend to be ringed by sprawling shanty towns. In industrialised countries, the decay of inner city areas is a cause for concern which redevelopment schemes have only partially addressed.

Lesson 1: DESCRIBING CITIES
What are cities like?
Children sometimes find it hard to distinguish between a city and a large town. Size is the key difference. Cities are large enough to have many different areas including business districts, suburbs, industrial areas and underground railways and airports. The photograph of New York skyscrapers shows how crowded inner city areas can become as the pressure on land drives people to erect ever higher buildings.
Mapwork *You might discuss with the children which regions and countries of the UK have the most cities.*
Investigation *Try to get children to include both good and bad aspects of city life as they complete this exercise.*

Lesson 2: WORLD CITIES
How are cities changing?
The world map shows that most of the world's largest cities are now the tropics or sub-tropics rather than in the mid latitudes. This is a trend which is likely to continue. So too is urban growth. It is estimated that three-quarters of the world's population could be living in cities by 2050.
Investigation *You might discuss the pattern which the world map reveals. How many cities are shown in the Northern as opposed to the Southern Hemisphere? Which continents have the most cities?*

The story of New York
New York, along with London and Paris, is one of a dozen or so well-established world cities that had a population of over a million people in 1900.
Mapwork *For an excellent street map of central New York go to www.arcgis.com*

Lesson 3: THE STORY OF LONDON
How has London grown and changed?
Cities develop from smaller settlements and flourish for a variety of reasons. London has benefited from its proximity to the European mainland. However, it is rather poorly placed as a capital for the UK. Rather than being in the centre of the country it is actually around 100 miles to the southeast.
Mapwork *Pupils might take a theme when they draw their London route maps.*
Investigation *This activity consolidates the mapwork on page 21 and requires children to conduct their own research.*

Copymasters *See 10, 11 and 12 for linked extension activities.*

Unit 5: JOBS

Factories make goods from natural resources or raw materials. They also assemble components or parts which have been made elsewhere. Usually we only see the finished product and are largely unaware of the process by which goods are manufactured or the jobs which are involved in making them. This unit introduces pupils to different types of work. One of the striking features of modern economies is that more and more people are involved in providing services. This means that it is increasingly hard to see how individual activities contribute to creating wealth.

Lesson 1: MAKING THINGS
Where are things made?

When you look at a factory from the outside there is little way of knowing what happens inside. This lesson explores the way that factories are organised and identifies some of the different work areas that are needed.

How do factories work?

The diagrams and text summarise the process of turning raw materials into products.

Mapwork *You could identify local factories by looking at an aerial photograph or map of your locality.*

Investigation *The notion of inputs and outputs provides a generic way of thinking which can be applied, not only to factories, but to a range of other processes.*

Lesson 2: DIFFERENT JOBS
How do people earn a living?

Many children have rather confused notions about what work actually entails. This study of a small harbour illustrates how a range of activities combine to running and operating a work place. The special skills which each person contributes are highlighted.

Mapwork *Pupils will have to imagine the overhead view in order to make the plan. This is an important mapwork skill.*

Investigation *You could extend the activity by getting children to think about the technology which helps each person to perform their duties.*

Lesson 3: TYPES OF WORK
What are the different types of work?

Two hundred years ago primary activities provided the majority of employment for people in the UK. Many people worked on the land or supported farmers either directly or indirectly. As the economy has changed so has the nature of work. Most jobs are now found in towns and cities. This has had profound effects on individual life styles, on where people live and the amount that they travel.

Mapwork *You could develop the mapwork activity by considering primary, secondary and tertiary activities in and around your school.*

Investigation *When the children compile their scrapbooks they might make up some jobs of their own to add to the examples they have already discovered.*

Copymasters *See 13, 14 and 15 for linked extension activities.*

Unit 6: POLLUTION

There is nothing new about pollution. The streets of medieval London and other cities were littered with rubbish and the royal court moved from place to place as sewage began to create a health hazard. What has changed, however, is the scale of the problem. In the last 50 years, industrial production has increased tenfold and human numbers have doubled. This has put the environment under immense strain. People are beginning to realise that the Earth is an enclosed ecosystem with a finite capacity but have yet to find ways of making significant responses.

Lesson 1: DAMAGING THE ENVIRONMENT

What causes pollution?

The Deepwater Horizon oil spill in 2010 illustrates how one single accident can cause terrible damage. It took 87 days to cap the well by which time 50 million barrels of oil had leaked into the sea causing extensive damage to marine and wildlife habitats. The legal claims resulting from the spill cost BP such huge sums of money there was a danger it could become bankrupt. As well as thinking about disasters, children need to understand that oil brings us many benefits. The problem is that they come at a cost.

How do we cause pollution?

The three 'talking heads' illustrate that we are all responsible for pollution in different ways.

Mapwork *The mapwork exercise is a reminder that pollution affects many different environments – not just places overseas.*

Investigation *Thinking about what will happen to things that we use in our everyday life is a reminder that we all leave environmental footprints and that we all have a responsibility to reduce the impact that we have on the planet.*

Lesson 2: 'GREEN LIVING'

How can we reduce pollution?

This lesson considers some of the ways pollution can be addressed. It also introduces the notion of renewable energy. It is important that children are not left feeling helpless in the face of pollution problems. Learning about current issues is the first step towards engagement and action.

Mapwork *The mapwork exercise may reveal hotspots, especially if litter and other forms of pollution are included.*

Investigation *Pupils could work in groups to devise their waste and pollution policy – the exercise is liable to generate a good deal of discussion.*

Lesson 3: EXPLORING CLEAN ENERGY

Can old power stations make clean energy?

Coal-fired power stations still generate nearly half the electricity used in the UK. Finding ways of reducing the pollution that they cause is a key priority in reducing carbon emissions. Using wood pellets may be one way forward.

A local investigation

Making a study of pollution in and around the school grounds will alert pupils to local problems at a scale which they can understand.

Mapwork *There are opportunities for pupils to record their findings electronically using GIS and other electronic mapping packages.*

Investigation *The investigation might stimulate debate about how local communities can contribute to solving problems and improving the quality of the environment.*

Copymasters *See 16, 17 and 18 for linked extension exercises.*

Information on the units

Unit 7: WALES

Wales has been politically united with England since 1535 but has retained many of its traditions and cultures. It has a population of just over three million people, the majority of whom live in Gwent, and Mid, South and West Glamorgan. Around one person in six can speak or understand Welsh. In the past most jobs in Wales used to be in mining and heavy industry but many factories have now closed. Self employment and tourism are increasingly important.

Lesson 1: MOUNTAINS AND VALLEYS
What is Wales like?

This lesson introduces pupils to Wales and highlights some of the factors which contribute to its distinct identity. There is a balance between physical and human geography themes in both the text and photographs. The map of Wales shows some of key features which children need to recognise for their locational understanding.

Mapwork *Children will need to use string or something flexible to measure the distance round the coast. This might lead to other coastline measurements such as the length of the Welsh coastline.*

Investigation *There are considerable differences between North and South Wales in terms of settlement, transport and work.*

Lesson 2: THE STORY OF BLAENAVON
How is Wales changing?

Blaenavon was built as a mining town to provide iron and coal in the Industrial Revolution. The way that it flourished and declined is typical of many other places in South Wales. Change is a major theme throughout this unit. As pupils learn about Blaenavon they will also be able to see how people have interacted with their surroundings. The story of the town would have been very different had minerals not been discovered there.

Mapwork *Pupils will need to access an Ordnance Survey map in order to complete this exercise. If this is not available it would be possible to make comparisons with Google maps.*

Investigation *When they draw their timelines encourage pupils to speculate about how Blaenavon might evolve in the years to come so that they consider its future as well as the past.*

Lesson 3: A VISIT TO BIG PIT
What was it like to be a coal miner?

Big Pit is on the eastern edge of the South Wales coalfield and one of a number of other similar mines in the area. All the deep coal mines in Wales have now closed but opencast mining still continues. Big Pit illustrates a way of life that no longer exists and now serves as a monument to the endeavour that made Britain a world power in the nineteenth and early twentieth centuries.

Mapwork *The spoke chart provides a visual representation of local attractions. Pupils might draw the spokes different lengths according to their distance from the school.*

Investigation *World Heritage Sites fall into two categories: they are either buildings and places which have been made by people or they are natural features. As they conduct their research it is instructive for children to think about why particular sites have been selected for designation.*

Copymasters *See 19, 20 and 21 for linked extension activities.*

Unit 8: GREECE

Greece consists of the land at the southern tip of the Balkan peninsula and numerous small islands in the Aegean and Ionian Seas. It is a mountainous country with strong agricultural traditions. The hot, dry summers and extensive coastline have made it popular with tourists. However, there are also environmental problems. Athens suffers badly from air pollution and the whole country lies in an earthquake zone. Political links between Britain and Greece were strengthened in 1981 when the country became the tenth member of the European Union. Cultural links date back to ancient Greek civilization which is the source for many contemporary ideas in science, art, politics and philosophy.

Lesson 1: INTRODUCING GREECE
What is Greece like?
You could introduce the unit with a brainstorm in which the children list all the things they know about Greece. They may already have quite a few associations and the exercise will reveal stereotypes and serve as a baseline against which to gauge their progress and development.

Mapwork *This exercise requires pupils to use a scale bar and will help to consolidate their understanding of distance.*

Investigation *You might help pupils structure their fact files by providing them with headings. Alternatively you might develop it as a literacy exercise.*

Lesson 2: SUMMER IN ATHENS
What is the summer like in Athens?
There are many children in Athens who live like Dimitra. Most families live in flats and in the summer nearly everyone sleeps during the afternoon to avoid the intense heat.

Mapwork *As an extension exercise consider why Athens was a good place to build a city. Possible answers are (1) the hills provided a defensive position above the plains of Attica, (2) Athens is in a good position for reaching the Aegean islands and different parts of the mainland.*

Investigation *Comparing timelines will highlight differences between life in Athens and the UK which you may want to discuss.*

Lesson 3: A GREEK ISLAND
What is it like to visit Amorgos?
Amorgos is typical of many Greek islands. It has a rugged landscape and small ports around the coast. There is also a monastery and some old windmills. The island has considerable conservation value. There are also archeaological remains which date back some 5000 years.

Mapwork *Children will have the chance to reflect on the distinct characteristics of Amorgos as they make their own maps.*

Investigation *Thinking about what Dimitra might say about Athens and Amorgos is an exercise which requires children to combine their geographical understanding with a sense of empathy and is an effective way of challenging stereotyes.*

Copymasters *See 22, 23 and 24 for linked extension exercises.*

Information on the units

Unit 9: NORTH AMERICA

North America has a number of distinct geographical regions. One of them, the Caribbean, consists of hundreds of tropical islands the largest of which are Cuba and Hispanola. Many of the islands are of volcanic origin and rise to considerable heights. Others are much flatter coral reefs or cays (small, sandy islands above coral reefs). The Caribbean has a unique mixture of cultures and population. Many people are descended from Africans who were brought as brought as slaves to work on sugar and cotton plantations. The Caribbean is also a bio-diversity hotspot with a rich variety of plants and creatures including extensive coral reefs. However, deforestation, pollution and encroachment have caused considerable damage.

Lesson 1: INTRODUCING THE CARIBBEAN
What is the Caribbean like?

Most children will already have images of the Caribbean so you might begin by exploring their ideas. Use the photographs and text on pages 50-51 to expand these notions and set the scene for a more in-depth study.

Mapwork *See that the children understand that the Tropics are those parts of the world where the sun is directly overhead at least once a year. The atlas research will help them to see links between different parts of the world which have similar climates.*

Investigation *Severe tropical storms affect all areas of the Tropics. They are called hurricanes in the Caribbean, cyclones in the Indian Ocean and typhoons in the Pacific.*

Lesson 2: FINDING OUT ABOUT JAMAICA
What is Jamaica like?

This lesson and the one that follows it focus on Jamaica. The country is small enough for junior school children to make sense of its physical and human characteristics. In addition there are many people living in Britain today who have connections with Jamaica. This makes it a particularly relevant case study.

Mapwork *The mapwork exercise asks pupils to find out about other Caribbean islands. If they each selected a different island, they could combine their results in a class display.*

Investigation *Jamaica has strong links with the UK. As well as thinking geographically, pupils might want to explore other dimensions such as history, music, art and literature.*

Lesson 3: LIVING IN JAMAICA
How is Jamaica changing?

Eunice Grant provides a very personal account of her life in Jamaica. Inevitably her experience is limited and individual. However, personal portraits of this kind have the advantage of being both detailed and authentic. You may find you are able to locate someone such as a friend or parent who can also talk about their life in Jamaica which will enable the lesson to develop into a more substantial study.

Mapwork *Using data about tourist visits, get the children to mark the countries where most tourists to Jamaica come from on a world map.*

Investigation *Pupils might use the facts they have assembled to create a quiz about Jamaica for children in other classes.*

Copymasters *See 25, 26 and 27 for linked extension exercises.*

Information on the units

Unit 10: AFRICA

Much of Africa consists of old, hard rocks which have been covered by sand and other sediments. The continent can be divided into two parts. In the north and west there is a vast low-lying plateau which includes the Sahara Desert. To the south and east there is a much higher plateau which is the source of most of the main rivers. Africa has abundant natural resources and a small population in relation to its size. However, a mixture of colonialism, slavery and cash crop agriculture have taken their toll. Today, large numbers of people live in poverty without adequate food, safe water or schools. International efforts such as the United Nations Millennium Development Goals have attempted to address these problems but achieved limited results. More fundamental reforms of international trade and finance might help to bring about greater peace and political stability.

Lesson 1: INTRODUCING AFRICA
What is Africa like?

Many children think about Africa as a single country rather than as a continent. They also tend to have negative images of Africa which they may have gleaned from the media and advertisements. It is important to challenge such ideas. Stressing positive aspects of African life alongside contemporary economic realities can help to create more balanced images. Stories, music, art and festivals are all good starting points which celebrate cultural achievements. Learning about physical geography can amplify such studies in a neutral way and lead to a more in-depth understanding of different places.

Mapwork *This exercise will help pupils learn about African countries through a focus on vegetation and biomes.*

Investigation *Children might work in groups and pool their ideas as they discuss the questions for the quiz.*

Lesson 2: KENYA
Finding out about Kenya

Miriam's letter, the map of Kamosong and the items on the display table all provide first-hand information about life in Kenya. Artefacts of all kinds can be a particularly valuable teaching resource because they can be handled and used as evidence. You may be surprised to find that you can build up your own collection using items from local shops and supermarkets. Pupils too can be invited to contribute items to any display. When set alongside photographs and commercially produced study packs there should no shortage of resources for pupils to interrogate.

Mapwork *Finding out about air routes from London to Nairobi will help to set this lesson in context.*

Investigation *The similarities between lives in very different parts of the world is one of the conclusions which might emerge from this activity.*

Lesson 3: LIVING IN KENYA
How is Kenya changing?

Like most countries all over the world Kenya is changing fast. The growth of cities and pressure on the environment are universal themes. The way that people are responding to these challenges is part of geography. Presenting pupils with up to date information about what is happening will help to keep your teaching meaningful and relevant. This lesson looks to the future and could be supplemented by the latest news reports and internet searches.

Mapwork *Annotating a map is a generic skill which pupils can practice in this exercise.*

Investigation *There is a danger that children will get carried away by the design process as they make their advertisements so see that they remember to focus on geographical information.*

Copymasters *See 28, 29 and 30 for linked extension exercises*

Copymaster matrix

Unit	Copymaster	Description
Seas and oceans	1 Beneath the surface	The children complete drawings and describe plants and animals at different ocean levels.
	2 The ocean environment	Pupils create a 'picture tower' about different ocean threats.
	3 Learning about seas	An exercise to identify oceans and seas on a world map.
Wearing away the land	4 Rivers in action	The children colour drawings of erosion, transportation and deposition and put them in order.
	5 Preventing flood damage	Pupils link drawings and descriptions of flood prevention measures.
	6 Finding out about rivers	The children draw some river surveying equipment and say how it is used
The seasons	7 Changing seasons	The children draw a tree in the four different seasons and name seasonal clues.
	8 Seasons worldwide	Children compile a rainfall graph for Rome and compare it to London.
	9 Seasonal influences	The children find out how school activities are affected by summer and winter weather.
Cities	10 Describing cities	The children complete pictures and speech bubbles about city life.
	11 World cities	An exercise to name and locate cities on a world map.
	12 The story of London	Pupils link complete drawings of different London buildings and sort them into categories.
Jobs	13 Making things	The children create a land use map of a factory using colours specified in a key.
	14 Different jobs	Pupils consider the different jobs done in a harbour and decide if they would like to do it or not.
	15 Types of work	An exercise to reinforce the difference between primary, secondary and tertiary activity.

Aim	Teaching point
To show how the ocean changes at different levels.	Discuss how the light, temperature and pressure change with the depth of water.
To illustrate how the oceans are important to us in a variety of ways.	Pupils will need glue and scissors for this activity.
To reinforce locational knowledge about oceans and seas.	This activity could be used to support the mapwork exercise on page 6.
To show that erosion, transportation and deposition are part of a sequence.	Talk about the different processes before using this copymaster.
To consider the effectiveness of different strategies for preventing floods.	See that pupils understand the specialist terms like 'levees' and 'cut-offs' before they start on this activity.
To illustrate different types of river surveying equipment.	The children need to write precise descriptions under their pictures.
To emphasise the different characteristics of each season.	Extend the work by asking the children which season they prefer and read seasonal poems.
To contrast UK and Mediterranean climates using climate data.	Check that pupils understand that the graph shows monthly figures that they need to represent in the columns.
To illustrate the effect of weather on human activity	Discuss the examples the children might use before they begin the sheet.
To show that people have different needs and priorities.	The children will have to infer if each person likes or dislikes the city from what they say.
To develop locational knowledge about cities around the world.	As an extension activity, the children could add other cities to the map using an atlas.
To consider the different functions and facilities in a major city.	See that pupils realise that each building may perform more than one function.
To introduce pupils to land use maps using a large scale example.	Talk about the way that different activities are grouped together in the key before pupils start this activity.
To illustrate the range of work opportunities in a single work environment.	You could widen this activity by considering the range of jobs (both direct and indirect) needed to run your school.
To show that there are major categories of work and that not all work results in a tangible product.	Children could use their own examples of different jobs as well as the examples in the pupil book.

Copymaster matrix

Unit	Copymaster	Description
Pollution	16 Damaging the environment	A snakes and ladders game based on environmental themes.
	17 'Green living'	The children draw pictures and write descriptions of the different ways of reducing pollution.
	18 Exploring clean energy	A survey sheet which children can use for studying local pollution problems.
Wales	19 Mountains and valleys	The children locate key rivers, mountains and settlements on a map of Wales.
	20 The story of Blaenavon	Children colour and analyse a cross section diagram of a coal mine.
	21 A visit to Big Pit	The children make a tourist leaflet for Big Pit.
Greece	22 Introducing Greece	The children add colour, titles and descriptions to four pictures showing different aspects of Greece.
	23 Summer in Athens	Pupils conduct a survey of twelve other children to see if they would prefer to live in the town or country.
	24 A Greek island	The children complete a simple picture diary of Dimitra's visit to Amorgos.
North America	25 Introducing the Caribbean	Children identify and label key islands, countries and seas in the Caribbean.
	26 Finding out about Jamaica	The children complete a map of Jamaica and make drawings of two different scenes.
	27 Living in Jamaica	Pupils make drawings to show change and environmental stress.
Africa	28 Introducing Africa	Pupils add information to a blank outline map of Africa.
	29 Kenya	Children compile a year book entry with facts and figures about Kenya.
	30 Living in Kenya	An activity in which pupils devise a 'kite diagram' about Kenyan life.

Aim	Teaching point
To introduce pollution problems and solutions in a lighthearted manner.	See that pupils understand how the snakes and ladders are linked to real world issues.
To help children realise they can help reduce pollution through their own actions.	Some pupils may need help when they explain how each activity reduces pollution.
To promote local fieldwork and investigation.	Identify safe places where children can complete the survey or set it for homework.
To consolidate points of reference on a map of Wales.	See that pupils do not obscure the labels and symbols when they colour the map.
To show how coal is often buried deep beneath other rock strata.	Talk with pupils about how the mine works either before or during this activity.
To extract and summarise information from a text passage.	The children will need scissors and crayons/felt tips to complete this activity.
To reinforce understanding of different geographical themes. To consolidate the portrait of life on a Greek island.	Get the pupils to arrange their drawings around a map of Greece as an extension exercise.
To explore attitudes to urban and rural life.	Introduce this activity with a class discussion so that pupils give considered responses when they complete the survey.
To create a visual portrait of life in a Greek island.	Pupils should draw on the text, photographs, maps and descriptions.
To introduce pupils to the geographical setting and context of the Caribbean region.	Blue outline shading around the islands and coasts will help to make the maps both clearer and more effective.
To familiarise children with different aspects of Jamaica.	Pupils could refer to any of the photographs in this unit when they make their drawings.
To illustrate some of the pros and cons surrounding modern developments.	Discuss with the children who benefits from change and whether everyone benefits equally.
To introduce pupils to Africa through key physical and human features.	Remind pupils that Africa is a continent made up of many different countries.
To build a balanced portrait using different types of information.	See that the children understand the weather chart and the meaning of the different headings.
To highlight contrasting and complementary aspects of recent changes.	You might get children to work in groups to discuss what they think about recent changes.

1 Beneath the surface

1. In the empty boxes draw the plants and animals which live at different levels in the ocean.

2. Write a sentence about each drawing.

Near the surface	
Below 500 metres Below 500 metres there are unusual fish like the Northern wolffish.	
On the ocean floor	

Make a 'picture tower' about the threats to the ocean environment.

1. Draw a picture in each panel below.

2. Cut round the edge, fold along the dotted lines and glue the box together.

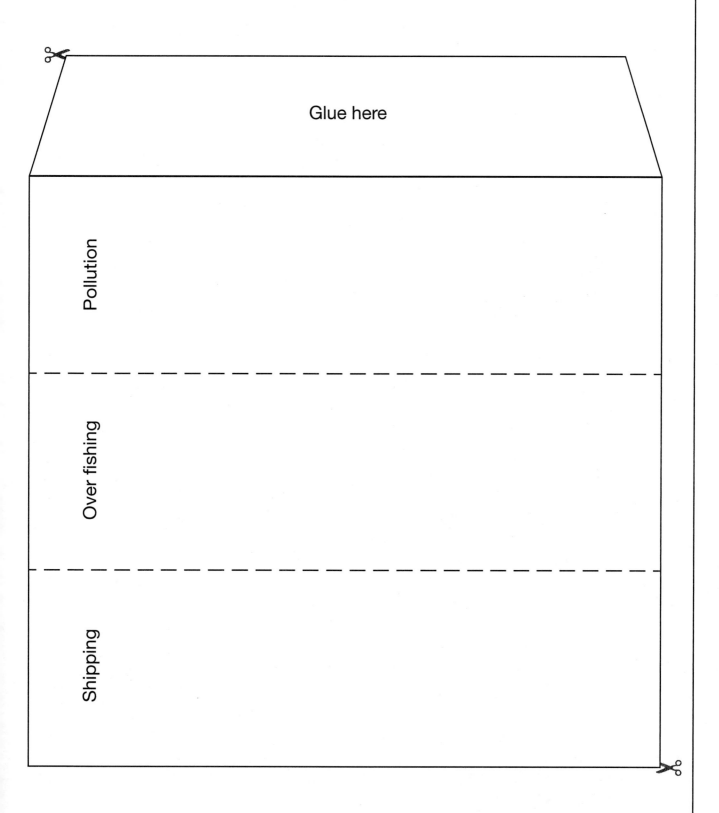

Glue here

Pollution

Over fishing

Shipping

③ Learning about seas

1. Write the names of the oceans in the boxes around the map.

2. Find where the seas listed in the table are on the map.

3. Decide if each sea is north or south of the Equator.

4. Write down the name of the nearest ocean to each sea.

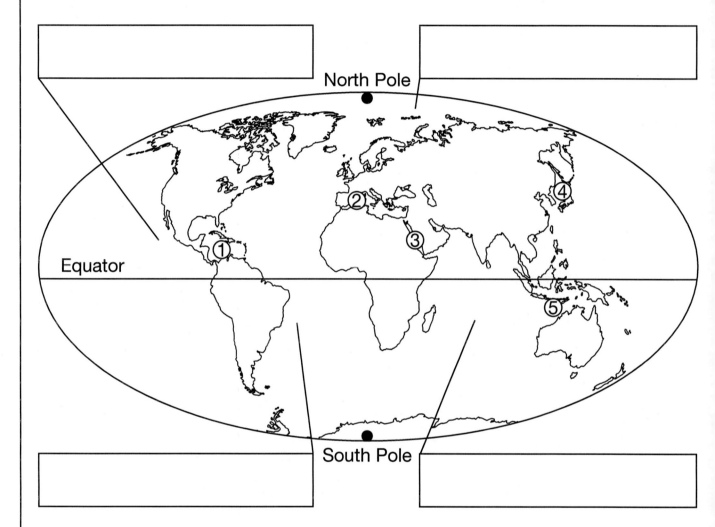

Name of sea	North or south of the Equator	Nearest ocean
1. Caribbean Sea		
2. Mediterranean Sea		
3. Red Sea		
4. Sea of Japan		
5. Timor Sea		

1. Colour the three drawings.

2. Write a sentence which says what is happening in each one.

3. Add arrows which link them together in the correct order.

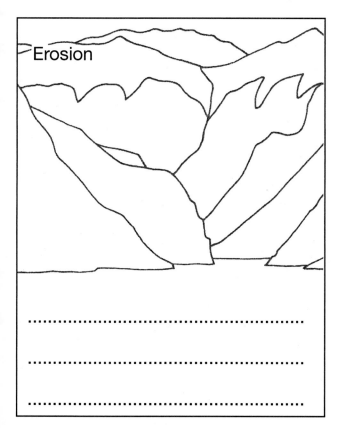

Erosion

....

....

....

Transportation

....

....

....

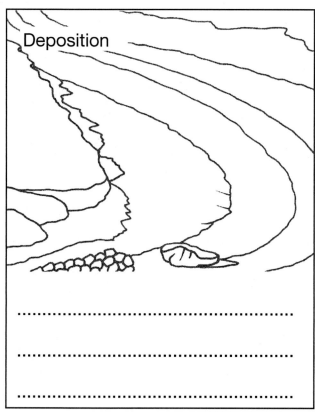

Deposition

....

....

....

Name ....

1. Colour the pictures.

2. Draw lines from each picture to the correct name and description.

	Dykes	New channels cut off some of the meanders so the water can flow faster.
	Levees	Dykes along one side of the river force the water to cut a deeper channel on the opposite side.
	Cut-offs	The sides and bottom of the channel are lined with concrete boxes to make them stronger.
	Boxes	Huge earth and clay banks hold back the flood water.

3. Say why some people think flood prevention makes things worse.

....

....

....

....

6 Finding out about rivers

Name ....

1. Draw the different pieces of equipment in each box.

2. Write a sentence which says what each one is used for.

Tape measure	Binoculars	Ranging poles
....	....	
Coloured corks	**Plastic bottle**	
....	....	
Magnetic compass	**Information book**	
....	....	....

1. Draw a tree in spring, summer, autumn and winter.

2. Colour the drawings to show the season.

3. Name one clue which tells you the season shown in each picture.

Spring	Summer
Clue	Clue ....
Autumn	Winter
Clue	Clue ....

1. Look at the table below. This shows average rainfall in London.

2. Colour the rainfall graph for London.

3. Make and colour your own rainfall graph for Rome.

4. What differences do you notice?

Rainfall in London

Month	J	F	M	A	M	J	J	A	S	O	N	D
Rainfall (mm)	54	40	37	37	45	45	57	59	49	57	64	48

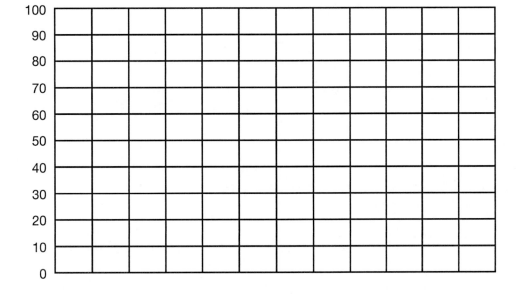

Rainfall in Rome (Mediterranean climate)

Month	J	F	M	A	M	J	J	A	S	O	N	D
Rainfall (mm)	61	52	39	42	49	28	18	27	70	90	95	70

9 Seasonal influences

1. Write down three things you do at school:

(a) in summer   (b) in winter.

2. Write a sentence which says how each activity is affected by the weather.

3. Draw your favourite summer and winter activity.

Summer

Activity	How the weather affects it	Drawing
1		
2		
3		

Winter

Activity	How the weather affects it	Drawing
1		
2		
3		

10 Describing cities

Name ....

1. Complete the drawings of people and the words.

2. Tick the box which shows if the person likes or dislikes city life.

There are lots of jobs in the city centre.

All the fumes from traffic are bad for my health.

Likes the city ☐	Dislikes the city ☐	Likes the city ☐	Dislikes the city ☐	Likes the city ☐	Dislikes the city ☐

There are no open spaces to play ball games where I live.

Likes the city ☐	Dislikes the city ☐	Likes the city ☐	Dislikes the city ☐	Likes the city ☐	Dislikes the city ☐

⑪ World cities

1. Name the cities which are marked on the map.

2. Colour the land and the sea.

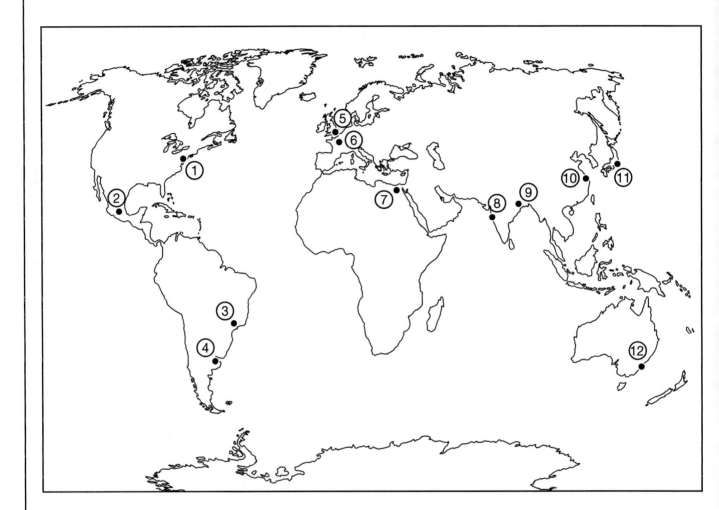

Name of city	Name of city
1	7
2	8
3	9
4	10
5	11
6	12

12 The story of London

1. Make drawings and fill in the names of the London buildings in the empty boxes.

2. Link each box to one or more of the circles.

3. Which place do you think is most important?

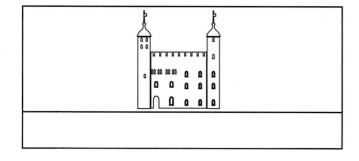

Tourism

Buckingham Palace

History

London Eye

Government

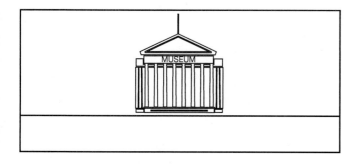

Leisure

Big Ben and Houses of Parliament

Art

13 Making things

1. Colour the empty boxes in the key below.

2. Colour the plan of the factory using the colours from the key.

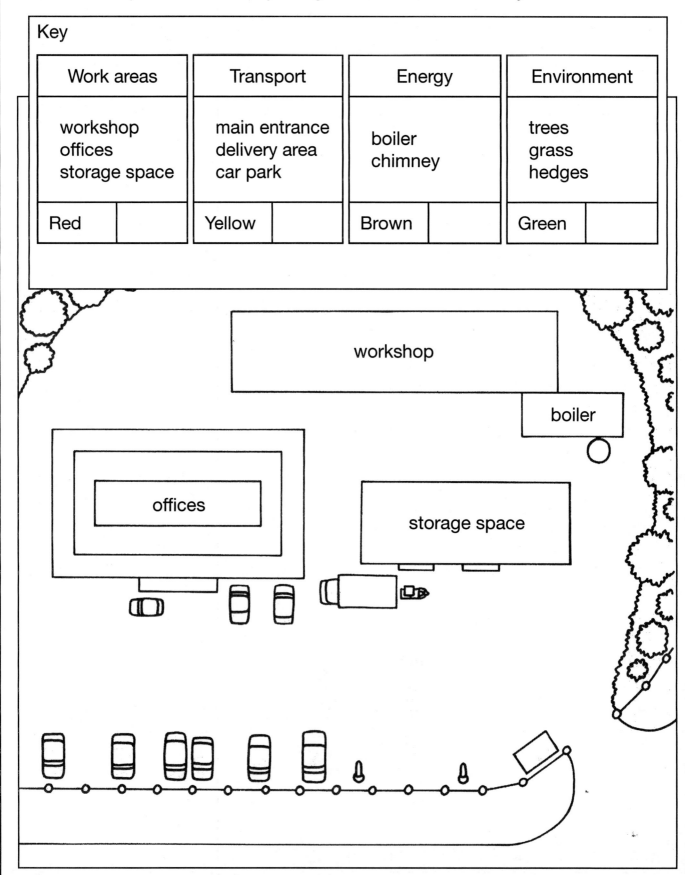

Key

Work areas		Transport		Energy		Environment	
workshop offices storage space		main entrance delivery area car park		boiler chimney		trees grass hedges	
Red		Yellow		Brown		Green	

workshop

boiler

offices

storage space

14 Different jobs

1. Describe the job which is done by each person who works in the harbour.

2. Colour one of the boxes to show if you would like to do that job.

Person	What job do they do?	I would like this job	I wouldn't like this job
Joan Lovell	- -		
Maria Archer	- -		
Bill Shaw	- -		
Steven Bell	- -		
Jack Seymour	- -		
Winston Hayes	- -		
Susan White	- -		
Andrew Knight	- -		

15 Types of work

Name ....

1. Make a drawing of one primary, one secondary and one tertiary activity.

2. Write a description of each job.

Primary activity Collecting raw materials	
Secondary activity Making things	
Tertiary activity Providing a service	

16 Damaging the environment

Name ....

1. Play this game with a friend. You will need a dice and counters.

FINISH	55	Dams drown farmland in China	53	52	Deserts spreading	50
43	44	45	Sewage pollutes North Sea	47	48	49
42	41	40	39	38	37	Area of rainforest saved
29	30	31	32	33	34	Global warming
Panda cubs born	27	26	25	24	23	22
15	16	17	Oil spill prevented	19	20	21
14	13	12	11	Lakes poisoned in Canada	9	8
START	More people use electric cars	3	New agreement to protect Antarctica	5	6	7

17 'Green living'

Name ....

1. Draw a picture of each activity in the empty box.

2. Write down how each activity reduces pollution.

Activity	Picture	How it reduces pollution
Recycling aluminium cans		
Making compost		
Travelling by foot or by bike		
Using 'green' goods		
Saving energy		

© Collins Bartholomew Ltd 2014

Primary Geography Pupil Book 5: Pollution pp34-3

Make a pollution survey in your area.

1. Think about each problem and circle one of the numbers.

2. Add up the total score.

3. Write a few sentences about pollution problems in your area.

Problem	No problem	Some	A lot
Traffic exhaust fumes	0	5	10
Factory fumes	0	5	10
Traffic noise	0	5	10
Aircraft noise	0	5	10
Polluted water	0	5	10
Litter	0	5	10
Overhead wires	0	5	10
Unpleasant smells	0	5	10
Factory noise	0	5	10
Vandalism/graffiti	0	5	10
Total			

0	50 or more

No pollution	Some pollution	A lot of pollution

....

....

....

1. Write these labels on the correct place on the map.

Cardiff   Swansea   Bangor   Snowdon

Cambrian Mountains   River Wye   River Severn

Anglesey   Bristol Channel

2. Draw in the mountains and colour the map.

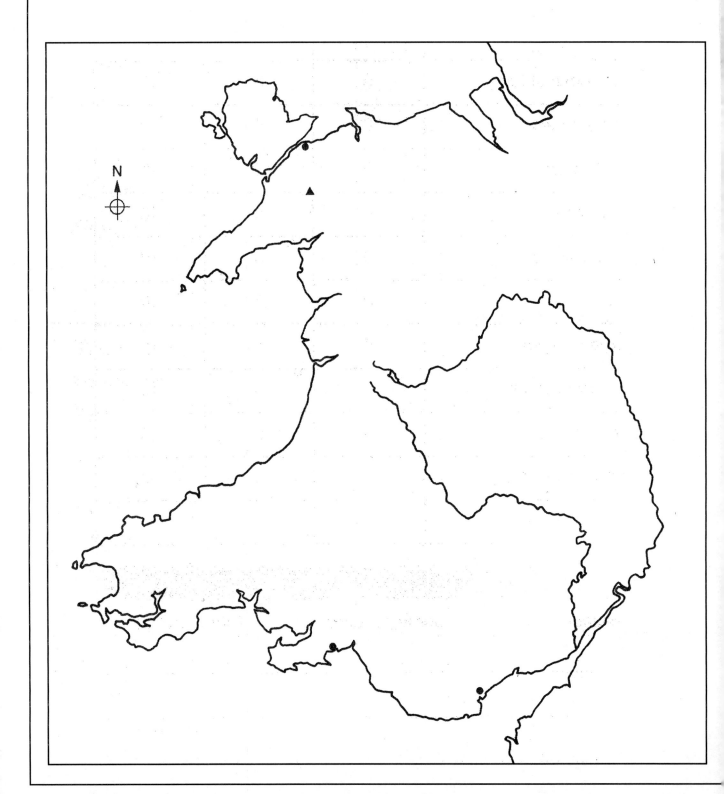

Name ....

1. Colour this cut-away picture of a coal mine.

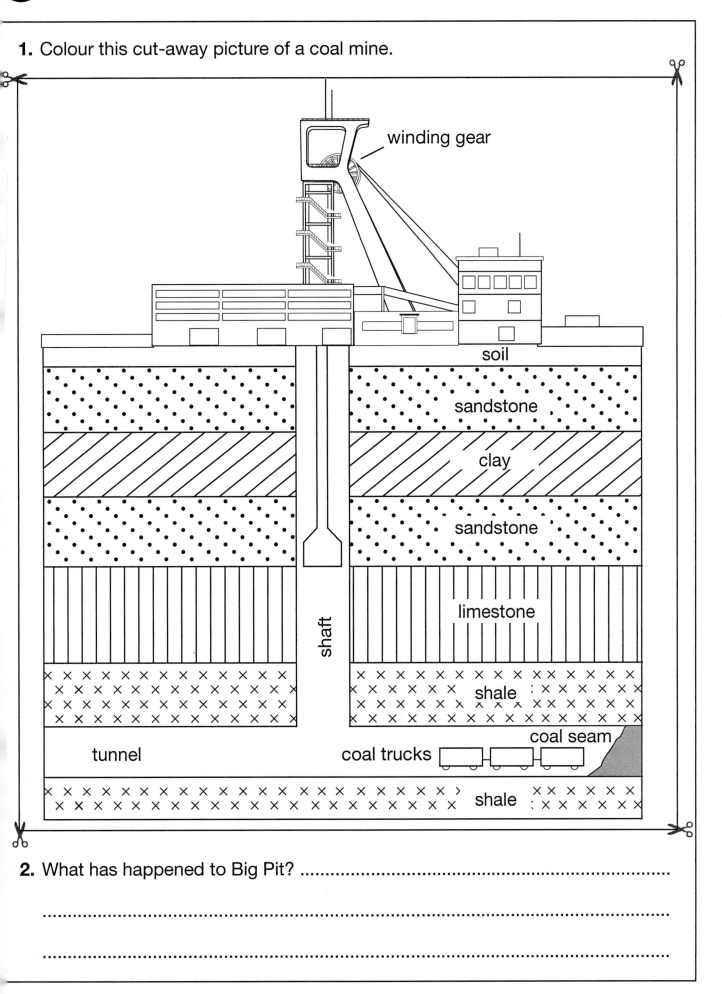

winding gear

soil

sandstone

clay

sandstone

limestone

shaft

shale

tunnel

coal trucks

coal seam

shale

2. What has happened to Big Pit? ....

....

....

Make a tourist guide for Big Pit.

1. Colour the pictures and the map.

2. Fill the empty spaces.

3. Cut round the edge and fold your guide along the dotted lines.

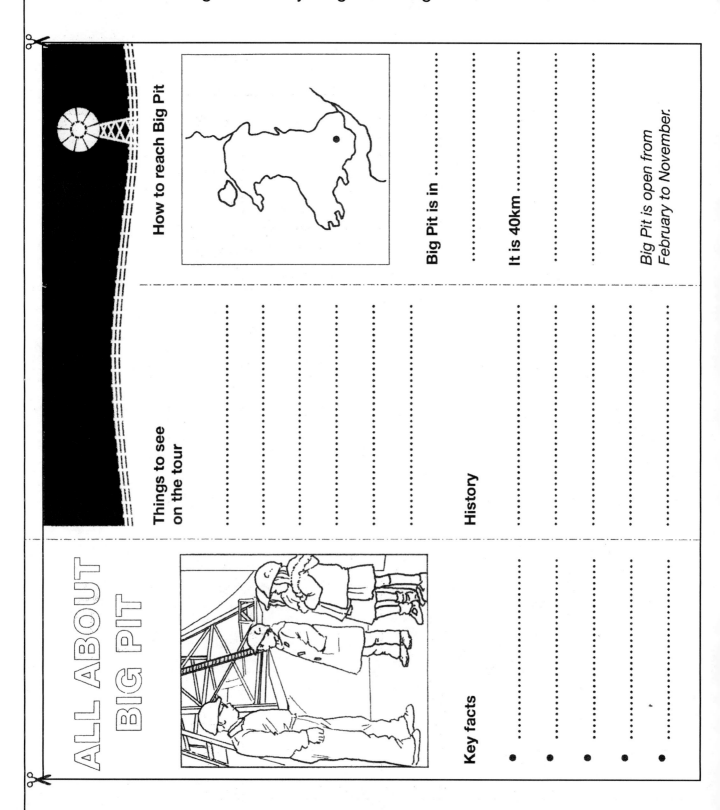

How to reach Big Pit

Big Pit is in ....

It is 40km ....

Big Pit is open from February to November.

Things to see on the tour

History

ALL ABOUT BIG PIT

Key facts

Name ....

1. Colour the pictures.

2. Write the correct title in the empty boxes

Landscape   Transport   Work   Settlement.

3. Write what each picture shows in the space underneath.

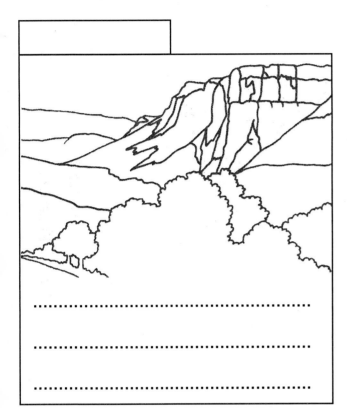

....

....

....

....

....

....

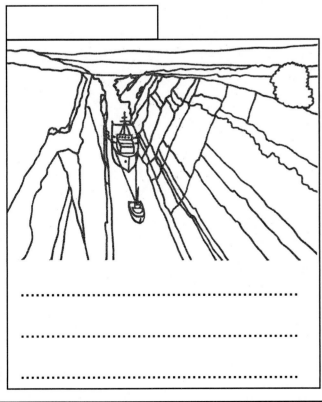

....

....

....

....

....

....

23 Summer in Athens

Name ....

1. Ask twelve children in your class these questions.

    (a) Would you prefer to live in the town or the country?

    (b) Would you prefer to live in Athens or Amorgos?

    Show their answers by putting a tick or cross in the table.

Name of child	Town	Country	Athens	Amorgos
Total number of ticks				

2. Add up the totals.

3. Tick the boxes to complete the sentences below.

    The survey shows most children would prefer to live a) in the town ☐

      b) in the country ☐

    The survey shows most children would prefer to live a) in Athens ☐

      b) in Amorgos ☐

1. Colour the drawing of the taverna.

2. Make drawings of three other things Dimitra would remember about her visit to Amorgos.

The taverna

1. Label these islands on the map:

   Cuba   Hispaniola   Jamaica   St Lucia

2. Label these countries:

   Panama   Venezuela   Colombia

3. Label these seas and oceans:

   Caribbean Sea   Atlantic Ocean

4. Colour the land and sea.

Name ....

---

1. Name the places marked on the map of Jamaica.

2. Make two drawings showing two scenes from Jamaica.

3. Write a sentence saying what each picture shows.

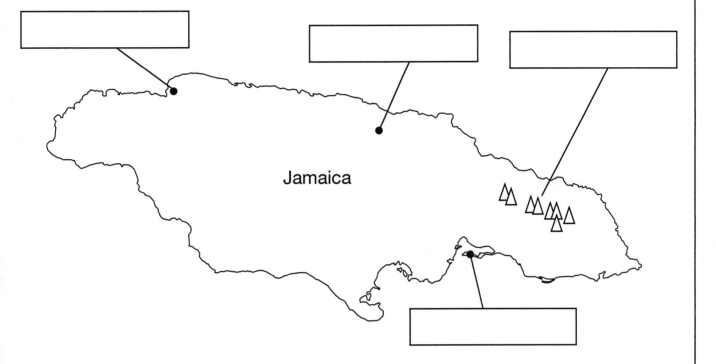

Jamaica

....

....

....

....

....

....

....

....

....

....

1. Complete and colour the drawings about how Jamaica is changing

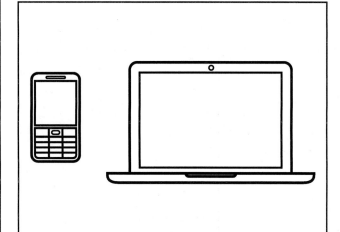

People have more possessions like mobile phones and computers

Parrots are losing their habitats

Tourists bring money to Jamaica

The mangrove forests are being cleared for buildings

2. Say in your own words how Jamaica is changing.

....

....

....

1. Mark the features and places listed in the table on the map below.

Rivers	Mountains	Deserts	Settlement
Nile	Atlas Mountains	Sahara Desert	Cairo
Congo	Mount Kilimanjaro	Kalahari Desert	Lagos
Zambezi			Cape Town

1. Complete the information and colour the maps and diagrams on Kenya.

Kenya

Population   25 million

Language   Swahili

Capital City ....

Other cities ....

....

....

Rivers ....

....

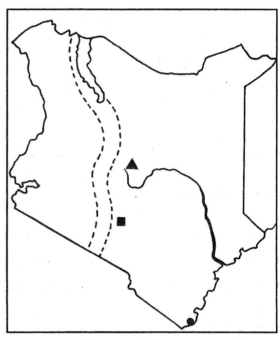

Map of Kenya

Landscape ....

....

....

....

Main crops ....

....

....

....

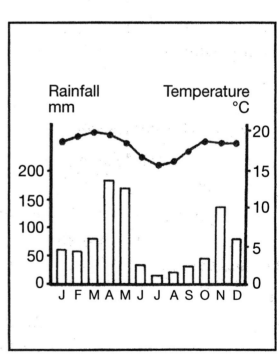

Weather in Nairobi

Name ....

1. Write notes and make drawings about how Kenya is changing on the kite diagram below.

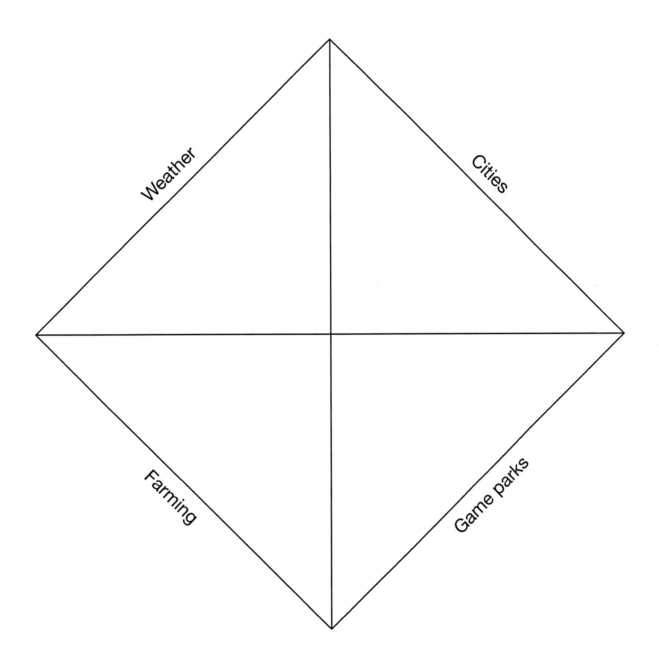

2. Which change do you think is most important?

....

....

....

Geography in the English National Curriculum

A new primary geography curriculum was introduced in England in 2014. This new curriculum provides a framework for schools to follow but leaves teachers considerable scope to select and organise the content according to their individual needs. It should also be noted that the curriculum is only intended to occupy a proportion of the school day and that schools are free to devise their own studies in the time that remains.

Purpose of study

The aim of geographical education is clearly articulated in the opening section of the Programme of Study which states:

> *A high quality geography education should inspire in pupils a curiosity and fascination about the world and its people that will remain with them for the rest of their lives. Teaching should equip pupils with knowledge about diverse places, people, resources and natural and human environments, together with a deep understanding of the Earth's key physical and human processes. As pupils progress, their growing knowledge about the world should help them to deepen their understanding of the interaction between physical and human processes, and of the formation and use of landscapes and environments. Geographical knowledge, understanding and skills provide the frameworks and approaches that explain how the Earth's features at different scales are shaped and interconnected and change over time.*

Subject content

The National Curriculum provides the following general guidance for each Key Stage:

Key Stage 1
Pupils should develop knowledge about the world, the United Kingdom and their locality. They should understand basic subject-specific vocabulary relating to human and physical geography and begin to use geographical skills, including first-hand observation, to enhance their locational awareness.

Key Stage 2
Pupils should extend their knowledge and understanding beyond the local area to include the United Kingdom and Europe, North and South America. This will include the location and characteristics of a range of the world's most significant human and physical features. They should develop their use of geographical knowledge, understanding and skills to enhance their locational and place knowledge.

Teachers who are familiar with the previous version of the curriculum will note the increasing emphasis on factual and place knowledge. For example, there is a greater focus on learning about the UK and Europe. Map reading and communication skills are also highlighted. On the other hand, there are no specific references to the developing world and sustainability is not mentioned directly. However, there is an expectation that schools will work from the Programmes of Study to develop a broad and balanced curriculum which meets the needs of learners in their locality. This provides schools with scope to enrich the curriculum and rectify any omissions which they may perceive.

Key Stage 2 Programme of study

The elements specified in the Key Stage 2 programme of study are listed below. The summary provided here should read alongside the statements about the wider aims of the curriculum. There is no suggestion that pupils should work to individual statements.

Focus
Extend knowledge of UK, Europe and North and South America
Location of world's most significant human and physical features
Knowledge, understanding and skills to enhance locational and place knowledge
Locational knowledge
Locate the world's countries
Use maps to focus on countries, cities and regions in Europe
Use maps to focus on countries, cities and regions in North America
Use maps to focus on countries, cities and regions in South America
Name and locate counties of the UK
Name and locate cities of the UK
Geographical regions of the UK
Topographical features of the UK
Changing land use patterns of the UK
Significance of latitude and longitude
Significance of Equator, Northern and Southern Hemisphere, Tropics of Cancer/Capricorn, Arctic/Antarctic circles, Prime Meridian
Time zones
Day and night
Place knowledge
Regional study within UK
Regional study in a European country
Regional study in North America
Regional study in South America
Human and physical geography
Climate zones
Biomes and vegetation belts
Rivers and mountains
Volcanoes and earthquakes
Water cycle
Types of settlement and land use
Economic activity including trade links
Distribution of natural resources including energy, food, minerals, water
Skills and fieldwork
Use maps, atlases, globes and digital mapping
Use eight points of the compass
Use four and six figure grid references
Use symbols and keys (including OS maps)
Fieldwork skills

WORLD MAP

WORLD COUNTRIES

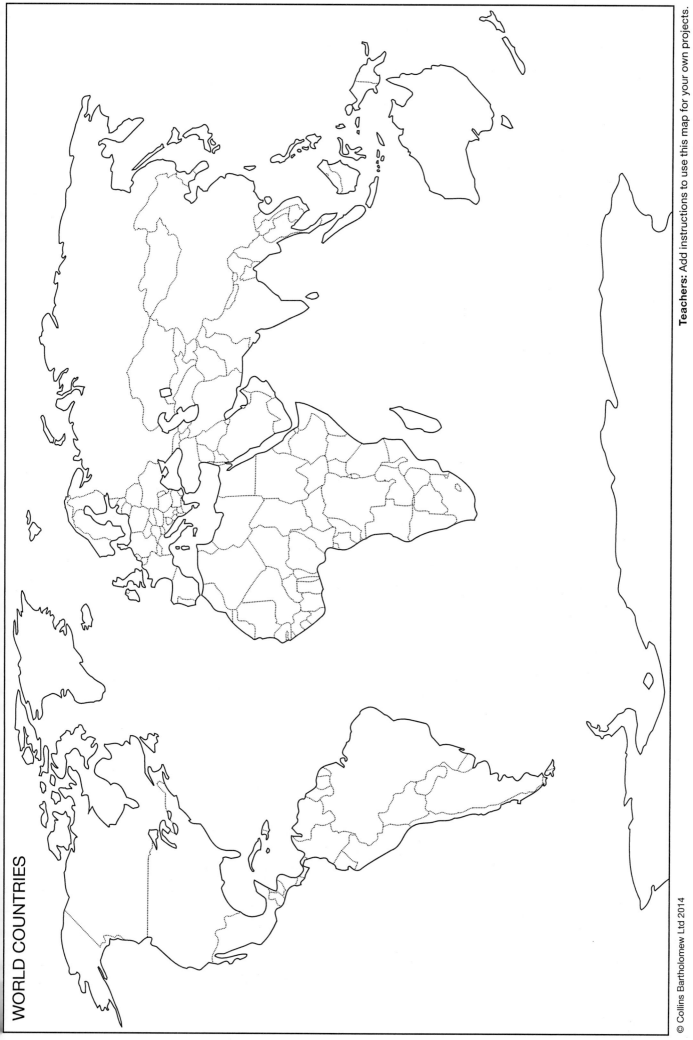

Primary Geography Teacher's Book 5
Collins
An imprint of HarperCollins Publishers
Westerhill Road
Bishopbriggs
Glasgow
G64 2QT

ISBN 978-0-00-7563661

Imp 001

British Library Cataloguing in Publication Data
A catalogue record for this book is available from the British Library.

Printed by RR Donnelley at Glasgow, UK.

Acknowledgements

Additional original input by Terry Jewson

Cover designs Steve Evans illustration and design

Illustrations by Jouve Pvt Ltd pp 34, 39

Photo credits:

All images from www.shutterstock.com